CRISISPOINTS FOR WOMEN

SO WHAT IF YOU'VE FAILED?

PENELOPE J. STOKES

NAVPRESS

A MINISTRY OF THE NAVIGATORS
P.O. BOX 6000, COLORADO SPRINGS, COLORADO 80934

The Navigators is an international Christian
organization. Jesus Christ gave His followers
the Great Commission to go and make disciples
(Matthew 28:19). The aim of The Navigators is to
help fulfill that commission by multiplying laborers
for Christ in every nation.

NavPress is the publishing ministry of The Navigators. NavPress publications are tools to help
Christians grow. Although publications alone cannot make disciples or change lives, they can help
believers learn biblical discipleship, and apply what
they learn to their lives and ministries.

© 1990 by Penelope J. Stokes
All rights reserved, including translation
ISBN 08910-93265

Cover illustration by Nicholas Wilton.

CRISISPOINTS FOR WOMEN series edited by
Judith Couchman.

This series offers God's hope and healing for life's
challenges.

All Scripture quotations in this publication are
from the *Holy Bible: New International Version*
(NIV). Copyright © 1973, 1978, 1984, International
Bible Society. Used by permission of Zondervan
Bible Publishers.

Printed in the United States of America

FOR A FREE CATALOG OF
NAVPRESS BOOKS & BIBLE STUDIES,
CALL TOLL FREE 1-800-366-7788 (USA)
or 1-416-499-4615 (CANADA)

C O N T E N T S

To Helen,
who had the courage to begin again.

ACKNOWLEDGMENTS

Thanks are due to a number of people for their participation in this project.

To my NavPress intercessors, Eleanor Lewis and Beverly Holden. They were faithful, invisible supporters who prayed for me during the writing of this study.

To my friend Jeanne, who encouraged me at several crucial points.

And most of all, to Judith Couchman, an editor of excellence, whose clear and specific direction made my job look easy. Thank you, Judy. An editor like you is every writer's dream. ∎

Have You Ever Felt Like a Flop?

Then you need this study guide.

Charlotte is a remarkable woman. She holds a position of high responsibility in ministry. She works tirelessly. She reaches out to people with deep love and compassion, and they're profoundly touched by her gifts and faithfulness.

But Charlotte often feels like a failure. Little mistakes devastate her. She's painfully aware of her smallest flaws, her occasional bad choices, her rare insensitivities. She sees her mistakes in microscopic detail, while her personal virtues lie light years beyond her vision.

Someone has said that it takes ten victories to compensate for one defeat; ten acceptances to balance a single rejection; ten affirmations of "You're okay" to override one critical voice saying, "You're not so hot."

Most of us readily agree that "we're not so hot." We're quick to acknowledge we're fallible, mistake-prone people. And we're slow to give ourselves the latitude we offer to others.

DEEPER PURPOSES

If you've struggled with big and small failures, if you haven't conquered the mistakes that follow you year by year, if you live with a vague sense of failure, you need to see there's hope.

And you need this study booklet. It can help you (1) understand the emotional and spiritual issues surrounding failure and (2) evaluate your mistakes and put them into perspective. Whether you study alone or with a group, you'll examine your mistakes in light of Scripture and grow to understand God's deeper purposes for your life.

The study is divided into several sections. First, the opening article, "But I Tried So Hard!" provides a foundation for understanding failure. The evaluation section, "Why Do I Feel Like a Failure?" encourages you to understand yourself. And five lessons present a strong biblical perspective on failure: your own and that of others.

You can't change the past, but you can change your feelings about it. You can alter how the past affects the present and change patterns that follow you into the future.

You'll never stop making mistakes. But you can learn to deal with failings without being devastated by them. You can learn to say, "So what if I've failed?" ■

—PENELOPE J. STOKES

But I Tried So Hard!

*Learn to deal realistically
with your failures.*

Out of the corner of my eye, I glimpsed a deer alongside the highway. My headlights gleamed in her eyes as she cleared the ditch and veered into the woods—inches from where my car skidded to a halt.

Shaken, I turned off the ignition and sat in the darkness, crying. I had avoided killing the doe and wrecking my car, but my life was full of a different kind of wreckage. And I knew it.

I was running away. Running from a long list of mistakes and failures that had decimated my spiritual and emotional life. On the outside, my life looked coherent, well-ordered, successful. I'd played the game well. I knew the right words and had convinced people I was "all together." But in reality, I was altogether falling apart.

An important relationship in my life had

broken beyond repair. My work was suffering; my emotional life was in chaos. In my Christian walk, the thrill of victory was fast giving way to the agony of defeat. I couldn't keep up the facade much longer.

That dark night, my close encounter with the deer shook loose a false image of my own success. I broke.

"I don't know what else to do," I told a friend. "I've tried so hard, and I've still failed!"

TRYING HARDER

A rental car company once used the slogan, "When you're number two, you've got to try harder." Many women have adopted that maxim for themselves. We spend our lives "trying harder" to be better wives, better moms, better workers, better friends. We see the image of Superwoman dangling before us like a carrot in front of a mule. And stubbornly, we struggle toward an unattainable goal.

Of course, there is nothing wrong with expending effort toward being and doing our best. But we set ourselves up for failure by establishing unreasonable goals, by holding onto unrealistic expectations for ourselves. Especially when we attain 94 percent of our goals and still call ourselves failures.

I've set goals like that. For many years, I taught writing at a small Christian college. Students often asked me for counsel and advice. Many of them responded positively to my input. But others never exhibited change or growth. They never responded to anything. They simply took up space, got their degrees, and returned home.

I suppose my record with students fared better than average. But the ones I couldn't reach bothered me. I didn't want to help some of them; I wanted to help *all* of them. And because of the few who resisted, I often fell into bed at night feeling like a failure.

A FALLEN WORLD

In his space trilogy, C. S. Lewis identifies earth as the Bent Planet ruled by the Bent One, who wants to distort the good given by the Creator.[1] We know the story as the fall of humanity, that fateful day when Adam and Eve disobeyed God and thrust our world into sin.

Since that day in the garden, mistakes and failures have plagued everyone. Daily, we live with the frustrating results of being human. In this fallen world, failure is inevitable.

Paul, the apostle to the Gentiles, experienced the same frustration. He lamented, "I have the desire to do what is good, but I cannot carry it out. For what I do is not the good I want to do; no, the evil I do not want to do—this I keep on doing" (Romans 7:18-19).

Paul described a dilemma common to all of us. We want to do right, but we can't seem to carry it off. Like trying to move around where someone sleeps, the harder we try to be quiet, the more racket we make.

If we hope to deal with our mistakes and failures—to cope without allowing them to destroy us—we need a basic assumption. That is, as long as we live in this world, we will make mistakes.

Many of us seem to believe that one morning we'll wake up perfect; that someday we'll conquer the threat of failure. But with that belief, our imperfections will devastate us. We need to acknowledge that failure is an inevitable part of human life.

IDENTIFYING FAILURES

"Well, yes, I know I'm doing some good things," Charlotte said when I tried to encourage her. "I'm getting some positive feedback. But there's this one person. . . ."

When I pressed for details, Charlotte couldn't give me any. There were no specific errors, no identifiable mistakes. But she had a vague, unspecified sense of inadequacy. She just felt like a failure.

Many women struggle with a similar, overwhelming sense of insufficiency. They can't point to any particular experience of failure; they simply feel like losers. These women usually struggle with deep issues of self-esteem, probably due to emotional deprivation somewhere in their lives. They feel just as guilty as those who've truly failed, and they equally need release from their prison of remorse.[2]

But even for true failures, real mistakes,

14

it's not enough to say, "Get rid of your guilt; stop feeling bad. You're only human." We must approach the real problem of failing with a real solution. And we must start by being honest with ourselves.

Some failures occur because of sin: disobeying the moral law and will of God. Others result from circumstance: the inescapable outcome of living in a fallen world. Some comprise errors in judgment: making wrong choices amid good intentions. Others are merely human foibles: the milk-spilling, foot-in-the-mouth kind of mistakes that seem earth-shattering but carry minimal long-range consequences. We need to understand the differences and the appropriate response to each.

Real sin: When he committed adultery with Bathsheba, King David disobeyed God's moral law. And that sin led to others: murder and deceit. While the results of David's sin lingered for a lifetime, his response to sin lifted the dragging weight of failure.

In 2 Samuel 12, the prophet Nathan visited King David to confront him. Faced with his wrongdoings, David neither justified himself nor minimized the magnitude of his actions. He said, "I have sinned against the LORD," and submitted himself to God's judgment (verse 13).

Yet the story didn't end there. While his son lay dying, David fasted and prayed and mourned. But when his son died, David got up and faced life. He knew the judgment of

God was complete. He didn't let the sin rule him forever.

When we fail because of sin, we need to respond as David did: face up, confess, submit to God, receive forgiveness, and then go on. Confession and forgiveness should set us free from guilt—not put more pressure on us. There is a freedom in forgiveness that can't emerge through denial or rationalization. And sometimes, ongoing self-pity over a failure can be as bad as the sin itself.

Outside circumstances: On the other hand, Job did nothing to cause the losses in his life. His "failure" was part of the larger, deeper purposes of God (Job 1:6-12). Friends tried to convince Job that he'd sinned, but false confession wouldn't have relieved his burden. He could only turn his eyes toward God and wait.

Sometimes circumstances create failure: a husband abandons his marriage; a crooked business partner embezzles funds and destroys the company; a friend betrays a confidence and ruins lives. We've no control over such situations, but often we accept the guilt and blame for them. We say, "What did I do to deserve this?"

Job could have asked the same question. Instead, he asked, "Shall we accept good from God, and not trouble?" (Job 2:10). He also declared, "Though he slay me, yet will I hope in him" (13:15). And thus, Job set a good pattern to follow when failure isn't our fault. He resisted accepting the blame; he continued to trust God; he waited to uncover the real facts.

Judgment errors: On the eve of Christ's crucifixion, when Peter pulled out his sword and cut off the ear of the high priest's servant, his intentions were clear. He wanted to protect his Lord. Peter wasn't evil, just misguided. He looked at the circumstances and reacted in the way he thought best. Right intention; wrong response (Matthew 26:50-52).

Many of our failures inhabit this category. We speak without thinking; we react without taking time to pray, consider, or evaluate. We want to help, so we blunder in and make matters worse. And afterward, when we see the person's severed ear and the look of pain in our Lord's eyes, we berate ourselves and vow never to draw the sword again.

When we make errors in judgment that hurt others or ourselves, we can acknowledge the mistakes, ask forgiveness, and learn from them. And realize that God looks into our hearts, at our intentions and motives (Proverbs 16:2). He knows the why as well as the what. And often He judges us much less severely than we judge ourselves.

Human foibles: The morning I arrived to teach my first college writing class, I wanted to appear relaxed and comfortable— the opposite of how I felt. I sat casually on the edge of the desk, smiling and chatting with the students. Then I decided to write my name on the blackboard. I swung my legs

17

over the side of the desk and jumped, feet first, into the trash can!

The minor mistakes we make, the egg-on-the-face slip-ups, can make us feel like fools—especially if we take ourselves too seriously. If our little mistakes hurt or embarrass others, we should make restoration. But most of the time, these blunders demand a nonjudgmental acceptance of ourselves and others, and a healthy sense of humor. If we can laugh at our own improprieties, we can relieve ourselves of unnecessary guilt.

BALANCING RESPONSIBILITY

Brother Lawrence, a seventeenth-century Carmelite brother, had a simple and singular perspective on his failings. *The Practice of the Presence of God* states, "When he had failed in his duty, he only confessed his fault, saying to God, *I shall never do otherwise if You leave me to myself; it is You who must hinder my falling and mend what is amiss. . . .* After this he gave himself no further uneasiness about it."[3]

Brother Lawrence wasn't flippant about sin. His intimate relationship with Christ demonstrated a commitment to holy living. But he understood a principle that we often forget. That is, sin is a fact of life, and forgiveness is offered freely through God's grace. Brother Lawrence had a no-nonsense, objective view of sin. Apart from God, he could do nothing but sin; with God, he could live forgiven of sin.

We need this balance. Some of us take sin too lightly. We say, "Oh, well, God will forgive it." Others carry the guilt long after we've sincerely confessed the sin.

We need to take sin seriously, but after confession, it's not necessary—or even spiritual—to keep flogging ourselves. Many times the load we carry is out of proportion to the mistake we've made.[4]

AFRAID TO FAIL

A popular book bears the title *Feel the Fear & Do It Anyway.*[5] The title attracts me. It speaks of risk and courage in the midst of fear.

Many of us fear failure. We avoid risks in relationships, in professional endeavors, and in personal growth, because we can't deal with failure. Our motto seems to be, "Aim at nothing, and you will always hit your goal."

We're afraid to fail because we tie *what* we do to *who* we are. We live in a society that values production. And if we fail to produce—whether it's books, babies, or bank accounts—we lose our sense of value. If we try something new and fail, if we enter into a relationship that doesn't work, if we blow it in our new job, or if our children get into trouble, we fear others will lose respect for us.

Objectivity about our mistakes isn't easy. But if we want to rise above the inevitable failures and setbacks of life, we need honesty with ourselves and others. We must quit playing the image game.

In 1 Samuel 15, King Saul made a mistake. Under orders to destroy the Amalekites completely, Saul disobeyed, saving the best of the stock for himself and allowing King Agag to live. When confronted with his disobedience, Saul could have repented. Instead, he made excuses for himself, asserting that he had obeyed the Lord and blaming others for his disobedience.

When the prophet Samuel removed Saul from the throne because of his disobedience, Saul replied, "I have sinned. But please honor me before the elders of my people and before Israel" (1 Samuel 15:30). From beginning to end, Saul felt more concerned about his image before the people than about doing God's will. He played the appearance game and lost, because "the LORD looks at the heart" (1 Samuel 16:7).

Keeping up appearances is a dangerous trap for Christians. If we're overly concerned about our image, mistakes will lead us into deception. We hide or rationalize our failures. But if we submit appearances to God and respond to Him in obedience, we'll walk away from the tyranny of images.

CIRCUMSTANCES VS. CHARACTER

In every way but one, Jeannine looked successful. She had a strong marriage, an important administrative position in a large college, an active and satisfying social schedule, close friends, and a deep spiritual life. But her daughter, deeply troubled emotionally, had attempted suicide and was hospitalized for psychiatric treatment.

Jeannine felt like a failure. No matter what else she had accomplished, she did not know how to help her own daughter. No other success could make up for it. But Jeannine made a mistake in her evaluation of the situation. She mistook circumstances for character.

Even if we invite failure and heartache by our deliberate sin, even if we've made bad judgments and unwise decisions, we still need to discern between actions and character. It is fair and healthy to admit "I have failed." But "I have failed" is a far different statement from "I am a failure." Failure is a noun that applies to events or circumstances, not to individuals.

"I have failed" is a statement of fact. When a relationship goes wrong, when plans fall through, when mistakes bring about hurt and mistrust, or when financial security falters, we may have failed. But failure is an event, a set of circumstances that can be dealt with and ultimately left behind.

To say "I am a failure" locks us in and denies the possibility of growth. It's a statement of character. No matter where we go, no matter how much we learn or change or mature, that failure will always follow us. We can't escape ourselves.

I once heard a story about a young mother's response to her son's misbehavior. When she caught him swinging from a coat rack in a restaurant, the mother reprimanded him, saying, "Bad choice, Jason. Bad choice."

That simple anecdote taught me volumes about the relationship between failure and self-esteem. Making "bad choices" does not mean, with God's grace, we're failures. If we can draw a distinction between what we do and who we are, we're better able to cope with mistakes and failures.

A PLACE FOR GRACE

Now the important phrase here is *with God's grace*. The Bible says plenty about our sinful natures and that "there is no one who does good" (Psalm 14:1). From the perspective of our inherent depravity, we *are* utter failures. We deserve to die. We'll never rise above the guilt of our sin. And for that matter, we'll never stop sinning.

But when we accept Christ and receive His forgiveness for our sins, we can view ourselves differently. Christ's cleansing blood washes away our guilt and shame (Ephesians 1:7). We can see ourselves through God's eyes: eternally pure and wholly acceptable.

So when we fail, we can view it as an experience rather than a permanent stamp on our foreheads. In God's eyes, His children are not failures. We can confront the problems honestly, take responsibility, learn and grow from our mistakes, and allow God's grace to meet our insufficiencies.

Our response to failure doesn't depend on whether it's major or minor; whether it's our own or someone else's fault; whether it relates to a specific event or a vague sense of not measuring up. Our response depends on whether we focus on ourselves *or* on God.

Focusing on ourselves takes a number of forms. We can become self-protective, refusing to take risks. We can develop an elaborate system of self-righteousness, denying that we make mistakes in the first place and blaming others for our difficulties. We can become self-consumed, eaten up with guilt for every real and supposed error. But each of these self-centered approaches has the same result: we do not deal honestly with failure, and we carry the weight of our past actions.

FOCUSING ON GOD

When we focus on God, the scene changes. He's in control of our lives; nothing lies outside the realm of His redemptive grace. Even when we make mistakes, fail in relationships, or deliberately make bad choices, God can redeem them. He doesn't always rescue us from their results, but He will use failures for our ultimate good (Romans 8:28).

God does not desire failure for us. Nor does He orchestrate mistakes to teach lessons or punish us. But He wastes nothing. He can use the worst experiences to clarify our spiritual needs and to draw us closer to Him.

We don't have to wait for the end of the

story to see God's purposes and to trust Him through our failures and mistakes. We can look to His character, knowing He desires good for us and His plan conforms us to Christ's image instead of our own.

In Romans 8, Paul makes an outstanding statement—a principle we can live by: "I am convinced that . . . [nothing] in all creation, will be able to separate us from the love of God that is in Christ Jesus our Lord" (verses 38-39).

Nothing can separate us from God's love. Past mistakes have been erased by the forgiving grace of God; present decisions are under His control; future struggles lie in His hands. We can rest on that truth and trust the outcome of our lives to the God who loves us—even when we make mistakes. ■

NOTES
1. C. S. Lewis, *Out of the Silent Planet* (New York: Macmillan, 1965).
2. These self-esteem issues are explored in another *CRISISPOINTS* study, *You're Better Than You Think!*
3. Brother Lawrence, *The Practice of the Presence of God* (Old Tappan, NJ: Revell, 1981), pages 15-16.
4. Sin, guilt, and repentance are the topics of the *CRISISPOINTS* study *Getting a Grip on Guilt.*
5. Susan Jeffers, *Feel the Fear & Do It Anyway* (San Diego, CA: Harcourt Brace Jovanovich, 1987).

Why Do I Feel Like a Failure?

Be honest about your big and little mistakes.

Don't be surprised if you hate talking about failure. By example and precept, you've probably been taught that life's ultimate goal is success: financial prosperity, lasting relationships, stable job opportunities, complete personal satisfaction, spiritual mastery, and so on.

In this study, you're going to break with that tradition. You'll need to be able to honestly admit your mistakes, because the first step in changing attitudes or behavior patterns is taking a look inside yourself.

The following questions will help you to begin to evaluate your feelings about past mistakes and failures. As you consider them, be honest with yourself. You need to understand what's really in your heart.

1. When you think of the words *failure* and *mistake,* what comes to mind?

2. What bothers you more: major failures or little things? Why?

3. Do you differentiate between big mistakes and small ones? Give examples.

4. a. What memories of past mistakes and failures still haunt you?

   b. Why do these issues continue to surface?

5. Are you afraid to reach out and risk because of past failures? Do you often take a safe route to avoid pain? Explain.

6. How else do failure issues affect you personally and spiritually?

7. Why do you want to study failure?

8. Complete this sentence: As a result of this study, the most important change I'd like to make is . . .

9. What trusted friend or family member could offer prayerful support while you're facing your failures?

10. Beginning this study, what would you like to tell God about your past failures and mistakes? ■

You've Got to Do Right

Begin to face the inner workings of failure.

Like most women today, you probably feel tremendous pressure to perform, to live up to the expectations of others.

Husbands, children, parents, friends, employers, and even church members want you to act or think in a particular way. And if you don't live up to their expectations, it's pretty stressful.

But "doing the right thing" in terms of people's expectations may be different from "doing right" according to the Bible's standards.

DOING WHAT'S RIGHT

1. In the following chart, identify what it means to "do right" according to each person listed. What are the results of those attempts to "do right"?

DOING RIGHT	THE RESULTS
Parent(s)	
Spouse	
Children	

DOING RIGHT	THE RESULTS
Friend	
Employer	

2. a. What effects, positive and negative, does trying to please these people have on you?

b. What feelings do you have toward them?

3. a. What do these verses indicate about your ability to "do right"?

Romans 3:10-12

Romans 3:23

Romans 8:1-4

Romans 9:14-16

b. How do you feel about these verses?

GETTING GOD'S HELP

The Bible says people can't do right on their own. In other words, we're all sinners. But as a child of God, you can depend on Him to help you do what's right according to His Word.

4. In the following verses, what are positive reasons to do right according to God's standard?

Exodus 19:5

Deuteronomy 11:26-28

1 Samuel 15:22

Jeremiah 7:23

5. What resources are available to help you
do right in God's eyes?

Psalm 119:9-11

Acts 5:32

Galatians 6:1-2

FEARING GOD AND OTHERS

6. a. In the following chart, compare your
desires to obey God and to please

people. What are positive and negative reasons for each?

POSITIVE REASONS	NEGATIVE REASONS
God	
People	

b. Are any of these desires to please based on fear? Explain.

7. What does the Bible say about fearing God and fearing people?

Psalm 27:1

Psalm 103:12

Proverbs 15:33

Proverbs 29:25

Galatians 1:10

FACING YOUR FEARS

An appropriate fear of God is based on love, respect, and reverence for Him. It is not a fear of His ridicule, disapproval, or condemnation. However, a fear of people is based on all of these and more. Unfortunately, you can mistakenly fear God for the same reasons you fear people.

8. a. Have other people's opinions ever made you afraid of failure? Has it affected your decisions? Explain, listing specific examples.

b. How did you feel about the outcome of these decisions?

9. Are there other reasons you're afraid to fail? List them.

10. Read 1 Peter 5:7-8 and 1 John 4:16-18. What is the source of a fear of man, a fear of failure, or an inappropriate fear of God?

11. What do the following verses say about God's attitude toward failure?

    Psalm 37:23-24

    Psalm 145:8-9,13-14

12. From what you've learned in this lesson, how might you alter your attitude about failure? How can you fear God instead of man?

This week, list the people, events, and circumstances that trigger your fear of failure. Then ask yourself:

- Why am I afraid to fail with these people or in these events or circumstances?

- How have I reacted?

- What can I do to change my unhealthy reactions?

Write a commitment statement that explains your resolve to change your attitude about failure. ■

Big Uh-Oh, Little Oops

Evaluate the magnitude of your mistakes.

Now I saw in my dream . . . that [Christian and Pliable] drew nigh to a very miry slough that was in the midst of the plain: and they being heedless, did both fall suddenly into the bog. The name of the slough was Despond.

Here, therefore, they wallowed for a time, being grievously bedaubed with dirt; and Christian, because of the burden that was on his back, began to sink in the mire.[1]

When you stumble and fall, it's easy to wallow in the slough of Despond and to think, if you just feel guilty enough, it will make up for your mistakes.

But feeling guilty is no more adequate penance than repeated prayers or walking on your knees to Jerusalem. Instead, you need

41

to understand the root of your mistakes and failures—and learn how to effectively deal with them.

THE FACES OF FAILURE

Human foibles: the embarrassing little idiocies of human life that make you feel foolish (F).

Judgment errors: the mistakes made when, meaning well, you choose the wrong decision (J).

Outside circumstances: situations beyond your control, where someone's decision or action, or natural consequences, result in your failure (C).

Real sin: actions or attitudes contrary to the revealed will of God that result in negative consequences to your outward life and inner spiritual condition. Sin can be:
- Nonhabitual violations of God's Word (S-1).
- Recurring or habitual sin (S-2).
- Addictions or spiritual bondage (S-3).
- Willfull, reckless rebellion toward God (S-4).

EVALUATING MISTAKES

1. Considering the list in the box on this page, evaluate the mistakes and failures of the following biblical people. (For example, "C" represents circumstance;

"S-2" indicates a recurring or habitual sin pattern. More than one category may apply to a situation.)

- Abraham passes his wife Sarah off as his sister (Genesis 12:10-20, 20:1-7).

- Joseph is thrown into prison (Genesis 39).

- Israel worships the golden calf (Exodus 32).

- Saul is rejected from being king (1 Samuel 15:10-12,22-23).

- The rich young ruler turns from Christ (Matthew 19:16-22).

- Peter denies the Lord (Luke 22:54-62).

2. Which categories apply to the following modern failures?

- Offering ham to the Rabbi's wife.

- Being fired because the boss wants a prettier secretary.

- Being fired because you came in late twice a week.

- Losing a friend because you flirted with her husband.

- Your marriage ending because your husband couldn't tolerate your faith.

43

- Forgetting the choir director's name on appreciation Sunday.

- Verbally or physically abusing your children.

- Losing your license because of drunken driving.

3. Think about the mistakes or failures that are uppermost in your mind. Using the same categories, identify the source of each error that haunts you.

ERROR	SOURCE

CONFESSING SINS

When your mistakes are caused by sin—either deliberate rebellion or unintentional

violation of God's principles—God will forgive
you when you confess them.

4. What do these verses say about confession and forgiveness?

   Isaiah 1:18-19

   Isaiah 55:6-7

   1 John 1:9

5. a. What keeps you from confessing sinful
      mistakes or accepting the freedom of
      God's forgiveness?

   b. What can you do about these barriers
      to confession and forgiveness?

6. How can you differentiate between seriously accepting God's grace or developing a flippant attitude toward sin?

7. If a failure in your life resulted from circumstances or another person's sin, how can you respond without bitterness?

Genesis 50:20

Matthew 18:21-22

Hebrews 12:14-15

8. Consider your failures that were inflicted by others. Then read Romans 8:28. What good could God bring from these failures?

9. If you've made errors in judgment that harmed or embarrassed someone, what steps can you take?

   Matthew 5:23-24

   James 5:16

10. How can these verses help change your perspective on mistakes and failures?

    Lamentations 3:31-33

Habakkuk 3:17-19

Romans 5:1-5

GETTING PERSPECTIVE

This week, transfer each personal failure you've listed in this lesson onto its own index card. Using the four categories, include the type of failure each one represents. Group the cards according to these types.

Then over the next month, deal directly with each sin: ask for forgiveness from God, others, and even yourself. After you have dealt with each item, tear up the cards and pray, "Thank You, God, that I'm now forgiven and free!"

To cement the forgiveness in your mind and soul, ask a trusted friend to witness your tearing-up session. ■

NOTE

1. John Bunyan, *Pilgrim's Progress* (Philadelphia: Lippincott, 1877), page 20.

Looking Good

*Separate performance from
your person.*

Life isn't easy. The formulas don't always
work. Even when you pray, even when you
commit yourself to faithfulness with God,
even when you "do right," there are still
unhappy endings.

To get beyond the fairy-tale image of
Christianity—to deal realistically with problems, struggles, and failures—it's crucial to
separate *who you are* from what you do or
what happens to you.

GATHERING EVIDENCE

1. a. How is God actively involved in His
      children's lives?

      Psalm 25:8-12

49

Psalm 139:1-16

Ephesians 2:4-10

b. What evidence do you have of His
   involvement in your life?

2. According to Titus 3:4-7, what is the
   basis of God's love for you?

MAKING CHANGES

Even though God's love for you is based on
His character, He desires to make changes in
your character.

3. How does God want you to live?

   Romans 12:1-3

   2 Corinthians 5:17-20

   Ephesians 4:15-16

   Ephesians 5:1-4,15-21

4. According to the following verses, what kinds of changes does God want to make in your life? Why does He want those changes?

Romans 8:29

2 Corinthians 3:18

Hebrews 12:10-11

5. According to Philippians 2:13 and
   2 Corinthians 8:21, who accomplishes
   these changes in your life? What is your
   responsibility in the process?

6. There's a difference between obeying God to be accepted by Him and obeying God because He already accepts you.

   a. Knowing God's love and intentions for you, why is it still easy to substitute religious performance for a relationship with Him?

   b. How can this become a performance trap?

7. Read Isaiah 1:11-14, 29:13-14. What is God's attitude toward religious activities done as the fulfillment of duty?

8. What activities are pleasing and acceptable to God?

Psalm 51:17

Hosea 6:6

Luke 10:38-42

Hebrews 13:15-16

INNER LIFE

Performance is a two-edged blade. It deceives you into thinking you're a good person because you're meeting other people's standards—or your own. But when you fail, your world shatters. That's because your self-esteem was based on what you *did* rather than *who you are*.

9. a. If God values your inner life more than your outward performance, how could that affect your attitude toward mistakes and failures?

   b. What steps can you take to stop depending on performance and start resting in God's grace?

REWRITING HISTORY

In Genesis 37–50, Joseph's life story was marked by experiences of "failure": enslavement, false accusations, imprisonment, abandonment. Yet the Bible clearly indicates that God was always with Joseph, giving him success in everything he did.

Read Joseph's story. Then rewrite his experiences, incorporating negative, fearful attitudes about failure. What would he say in certain difficult circumstances? What would he do?

Compare the two stories. What attitudes made Joseph's story a success? How did he contribute to his inward life when his outward life fell apart? How can Joseph's example apply to you? ■

Repeat Performance

What to do with the "I did it again" syndrome.

When you make the same errors over and over again, it feels devastating. The trust between you and others is broken. You even stop trusting yourself. The roots of your failures run deep.

Deeply rooted patterns can stem from deeply rooted problems. And often when you can't control your actions, you can plunge into debilitating behavior patterns, even addictions. Dr. Gerald May, in *Addiction and Grace*, says,

> *Then we will realize that we are our own worst enemies; we cannot beat ourselves. At that point, when we have exhausted all the available false repositories for our hope, it is possible that we will turn to God with a true sense of who we are, with an integrity that is both humble*

and confident, with a dignity that knows itself because it has met its limits.[1]

The first step in dealing with difficult behavior patterns is to acknowledge them. You can't resolve issues you refuse to confront. But once you face those problems, you can seek solutions.

REPEAT PERFORMANCES

1. a. How did the Apostle Paul struggle with recurring sin in Romans 7:14-24?

   b. In what specific ways do you identify with his lament?

2. What does Romans 7:25 indicate about the answer to Paul's question?

3. Considering Romans 8 as the extended answer to the question in 7:24, what factors help overcome the patterns of deeply rooted sin?

POSSIBLE PATTERNS

4. When you think about your mistakes and failures, can you pinpoint any repeated patterns? Are there common thoughts, choices, and actions that lead to the same failures? What are they?

5. a. According to the following verses, what could be the source of your repeat performances?

Proverbs 16:18

Jeremiah 16:12

Ephesians 6:12

James 1:13-15

1 John 2:15-16

b. Which of these reasons apply to you? What others could you add?

6. What is your common response to God over these repeated failures?

GOD'S FAITHFULNESS

7. What do the following verses indicate about God's memory concerning your sins and failures?

   Psalm 103:10-12

Jeremiah 31:34

Micah 7:19

8. If God forgets your sin, why should you be concerned about sinful patterns?

Philippians 3:13-14

Hebrews 1:9

9. a. What do you need to forget about sin that has been forgiven? What do you need to remember? Answer these questions in the following chart.

MY FAILURE	I CAN FORGET	I WILL REMEMBER

b. How can you keep the productive lessons and leave behind destructive memories?

10. a. How does your spiritual life compare to the biblical patterns of 1 Corinthians 13 or Galatians 5:22-23?

    b. What specific, habitual behaviors need to be changed?

11. How can these spiritual resources help you change? Use a concordance to find Bible verses that support your statements.

    Bible

Prayer

Worship

Fellowship

FIND THE BALANCE

As you deal with habitual patterns, you need a careful balance between your efforts, God's grace, and the Holy Spirit's work.

Permanent spiritual change does not come in a do-it-yourself kit; you must cooperate with God. Only He can work the internal changes necessary for a transformed life.

12. Write a prayer to God, describing (1) what you will do and (2) what He must do to root out your repeated sins and failures.

For the next few weeks, choose a nagging, repeated failure and chart your actions, attitudes, and any progress toward improvement. Your chart could look something like this:

Problem: Cutting other people down.

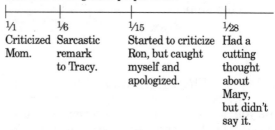

⅟1	⅟6	⅟15	⅟28
Criticized Mom.	Sarcastic remark to Tracy.	Started to criticize Ron, but caught myself and apologized.	Had a cutting thought about Mary, but didn't say it.

Before charting yourself, finish "The Incomplete Shalom Worksheet" on pages 79-80 to help clarify your goals for changing this negative behavior. ∎

NOTE
  1. Gerald G. May, M.D., *Addiction and Grace* (San Francisco, CA: Harper & Row, 1988), page 20.

MAYBE YOU NEED TO DIG DEEPER

Some of the problems you face cannot be dealt with alone. For example, certain repetitive and compulsive behaviors can be extremely difficult to overcome by yourself—or when you don't understand their deep roots.

The following questions may help identify issues in which professional counseling might assist your progress. Check the ones that apply to you:

❑ Does my life seem out of control with relationships going sour, overwhelming problems, continual crises?

❑ Do little problems seem like major obstacles to me?

❑ Have there been changes in my personal habits: eating, drinking, sleeping, personal hygiene, interaction with others?

❑ Are compulsive behaviors controlling my life: spending, sex, eating, drinking, gambling, other people's expectations?

❑ Do I struggle with depression—not wanting to get up in the morning, go to work, or relate to other people?

❑ Do I often feel unworthy of God's love and grace?

(continued on page 68)

(continued from page 67)

❏ Do I long for escape from my present situation? Do I feel any escape—even death—would be preferable to staying where I am?

For a specific recurring problem, you'll also want to answer these questions:

❏ Is this behavior extremely difficult to change? Why?

❏ Do spiritual disciplines seem *not* to help improve this problem? Explain.

❏ Is there a deeper, underlying problem—perhaps from a past wound—that aggravates this failure? Do I need spiritual healing?

❏ Is there a possible spiritual bondage that controls me in this area?

❏ Is this behavior an addiction?

If you answered yes to any of the questions, you may need help from one or more of these people: a friend, a pastor, a counselor, or a therapist.

First, be sure your helper is wise, godly, and informed about deeper spiritual problems. Then don't be afraid to commit to understanding, facing, and changing this behavior.

And remember: No problem is beyond the reach of the Holy Spirit's healing power. ■

Growing On

*Why you can trust God
and take risks.*

Christians don't ask why because Christians already know why.

Christians have all the answers.

Christians know the reasons for things because they know the truth.

Jesus is the answer; therefore nothing can be unanswered.

If Christians ask why, it's a sign of doubt; and Christians never doubt, so true believers don't ask why.

Oh, really?[1]

Any time you face the inevitable struggles of life, you have a choice. You can evaluate the situation according to circumstances: *If God loved me, this wouldn't have happened.* Or you can evaluate according to convictions: *I know God loves me, so He must have my best interests at heart.*

I don't understand, but I will choose to trust Him.

GOOD CHOICES

1. Psalm 37:3-7,23-29 encourages you to trust in the Lord. What are some results of trusting Him?

2. Why can God be trusted?

   Psalm 36:5-10

   Lamentations 3:23

2 Timothy 2:13

3. Regarding your mistakes and failures, what can you trust God to do?

BIBLICAL FAILURES

4. What do the experiences of these biblical characters reveal about restoration after a devastating failure?

Prodigal son (Luke 15:11-31)

Simon Peter (Luke 22:31-34,54-62; John 21:17-19)

Paul (Galatians 1:13-24)

/

5. In any of the above examples, was failure a key to future ministry to others? Explain.

6. a. From 2 Corinthians 1:3-6, how does suffering equip you for ministry?

   b. How might this principle be applied to your failures?

7. a. How can failure positively affect these behaviors? The Bible verses will add insight.

Judgmental attitude (Matthew 7:1)

Self-sufficiency (John 15:5)

Lack of compassion (1 Peter 3:8-9)

b. How has failure affected you in these or other areas?

c. What might be the consequences of not allowing failure to positively influence you?

FOCUSING ON GOD

Trusting God in the midst of difficulty is not a Pollyanna attitude that denies the reality of pain and frustration. It is turning your eyes away from God's hand (expecting Him to give you an escape from the problem) and looking at His face (acknowledging His loving care and wisdom).

When you focus on God, you admit your struggles and problems, but you also recognize and draw strength from the truth that God is in control, that your life is ordered by His power and protection. Ultimately, you can trust His character rather than your circumstances.

8. What do the following passages reveal about God's character? How does each characteristic apply to your life and desire to change and grow?

CHARACTERISTIC	APPLICATION
Nehemiah 13:2b	
Isaiah 30:18	
Isaiah 54:10	
Jeremiah 9:24	

CHARACTERISTIC	APPLICATION
Romans 4:20-21	

9. What changes can you make to focus on God's love and grace and to avoid focusing on circumstances?

TAKING RISKS

10. How can a knowledge of God's faithfulness and love enable you to take risks without fearing failure?

11. a. What risks do you sense God leading you toward?

    b. How might those risks fulfill God's plan for your life?

    c. Are you willing to take them? Explain.

READY FOR RISK

Don't let your progress end with this lesson. This week, begin the journaling exercises on pages 81-83 to help you face failure in the months ahead. ■

NOTE
  1. John Fischer, *True Believers Don't Ask Why* (Minneapolis, MN: Bethany, 1989), page 13.

The Incomplete Shalom Worksheet

An evaluation to help you set goals for change.

The title of this worksheet, "Incomplete Shalom," indicates that unaddressed problems and struggles interfere with your peace in Christ. It is designed as a self-help aid to evaluate major problems or struggles and to seek biblical responses. You can use a separate piece of paper for your responses.[1]

1. What is the problem or behavior pattern to be addressed? (Be as specific as possible; list one problem only.)

2. What reasons do I have for not changing? (Unforgiveness, hurts, etc.)

3. Why should I change? (List as many reasons as possible, including Scripture.)

4. What is my goal? (Give a general statement about what you intend to do.)

5. What could be my behavioral objective? How do I picture myself behaving? (Be as specific as possible.)

6. What is the process? How do I propose to bring about the change? (Be specific; be able to document.)

7. How will I evaluate the attainment of my goal? To whom will I give account? ∎

NOTE
1. Adapted from Rev. Paul Taintor. Used by permission.

Writing for Deeper Insights

Help yourself to start taking risks.

Keeping a personal journal is a simple and productive way to gain insight and to understand how God works in your life. A journal is not simply a daily recording of events, but an exploration into how things happen and what they mean—or how you feel about yourself and your life.

The one essential principle is that *a personal journal is absolutely private and confidential.* The journal is a place for you to be completely honest with yourself and God. And regarding this Bible study, it's a place where you can explore your feelings about failure and risk-taking.

God has a way of using the journaling to speak to you and to reveal new insights about yourself. Use the following questions and suggestions to begin writing, but don't limit yourself to just these ideas.

1. Write about your most devastating experience of failure. Face it objectively, as if you were a loving and compassionate friend responding to your struggles.

2. Write a letter to yourself, telling about your strong points and including specific ways you have helped and encouraged others.

3. What does faithfulness mean? Write about God's faithfulness and about the faithfulness of others.

4. Write about molehills you've made into mountains.

5. Describe an experience that seemed traumatic at the time, but that you laughed about later.

6. Write about images: the image you try to project; the image other people have of you; the image you see in the mirror; the images you have of others; the ideal image you have for yourself; the image of Christ.

7. Describe yourself, telling what kind of a person you are, without mentioning anything you *do*.

8. Explore the area of personal growth you're most concerned about.

9. Write out confessions of failures caused by sin. Thank God for His forgiveness.

10. Face risk. What does it mean to risk? What risks have you taken, and with what results? What do you want to risk? What are you unwilling to risk? Why does risk scare you? ■

Take Another Look

Build an encouragement file.

For many of us, the feeling of failure may not be linked to specific, identifiable events or mistakes. We simply feel bad about ourselves, that we "can't seem to do anything right." Sometimes an "encouragement file" can help.

An encouragement file is simply a collection of mementos that give specific and deliberate praise. Some people like to use a file box. Much encouragement from others comes in the form of letters, so use a three-ring notebook to store them.

File letters, cards, notes from telephone conversations, and portions of journal entries. When you're feeling discouraged, encourage yourself by reading what other people have said about you.

Following are some suggestions for building the file:

1. Glean encouraging passages from letters you have saved.

2. Reproduce sections from your journal.

3. Write a list of your good qualities.

4. Ask a close friend to write to you about positive character traits she sees in you.

5. Copy passages of Scripture that have been particularly encouraging to you.

6. Write out words of songs that lift your spirits.

7. Write about ways you are changing or growing spiritually, including specific examples of the changes.

An encouragement file is not an ego trip. It is a way to get a more objective view of yourself, to see your good points and successes through other people's eyes. Always balance time spent in your encouragement file with time in worship, praise, or Bible study. ∎

Resources for Recovery

Books for further help and study.

Beattie, Melody. *Codependent No More.* New York: Harper and Row, 1987.

Brother Lawrence. *The Practice of the Presence of God.* Old Tappan, NJ: Revell, 1958.

Chisholm, Gloria. *Encourage One Another.* Waco, TX: Word Books, 1986.

Crabb, Larry. *Inside Out.* Colorado Springs, CO: NavPress, 1988.

Fischer, John. *Real Christians Don't Dance.* Minneapolis, MN: Bethany, 1988.

Fischer, John. *True Believers Don't Ask Why.* Minneapolis, MN: Bethany, 1989.

Hansel, Tim. *You Gotta Keep Dancin'*. Elgin, IL: David C. Cook, 1985.

Lewis, C. S. *Out of the Silent Planet*. New York: Macmillan, 1965.

MacDonald, Gordon. *Ordering Your Private World*. Nashville, TN: Thomas Nelson, 1984.

MacDonald, Gordon. *Rebuilding Your Broken World*. Nashville, TN: Thomas Nelson, 1988.

May, Gerald G. *Addiction and Grace*. San Francisco, CA: Harper & Row, 1988.

Peterson, Eugene H. *Run With the Horses*. Downers Grove, IL: InterVarsity Press, 1983.

Shaw, Luci. *God in the Dark*. Grand Rapids, MI: Zondervan, 1990.

Stokes, Penelope J. *Grace Under Pressure*. Colorado Springs, CO: NavPress, 1989. ■

A U T H O R

Penelope J. Stokes, Ph.D., professor of writing and literature for twelve years, left college teaching in 1985 to pursue full-time freelance writing and editing.

Nurtured in her Christian faith by the Navigator ministry, Dr. Stokes has been active in Bible teaching and discipling for many years. Her writing has appeared in *Discipleship Journal* and other magazines.

She has also published five books, including *Grace Under Pressure* and an updated edition of E. M. Bounds' classic, *Power Through Prayer*. ∎

OTHER TITLES IN THIS SERIES

Additional *CRISISPOINTS* Bible studies include:

Getting a Grip on Guilt by Judith Couchman. Learn to live a life free from guilt.

Nobody's Perfect, So Why Do I Try to Be? by Nancy Groom. Get over the need to do everything right.

What to Do When You Can't Get Along by Gloria Chisholm. How to resolve conflict according to the Bible.

When Your Marriage Disappoints You by Janet Chester Bly. Hope and help for improving your marriage.

You're Better Than You Think! by Madalene Harris. How to overcome shame and develop a healthy self-image.

These studies can be purchased at a Christian bookstore. Or order a catalog from NavPress, Customer Services, P. O. Box 6000, Colorado Springs, CO 80934. Or call 1-800-366-7788 for information. ∎